DEDICATION PAGE

Dedicated to all those who want to be and to those who have found how great they truly are.

With special thanks to my late mother, Brenda Marie Kelly, for enabling this book and my prior to happen. Thanks as well to my family and numerous friends for their encouragement and anticipation.

-- KAG

AuthorHouse™
1663 Liberty Drive
Bloomington, IN 47403
www.authorhouse.com
Phone: 833-262-8899

Because of the dynamic nature of the Internet, any web addresses or links contained in this book may have changed
since publication and may no longer be valid. The views expressed in this work are solely those of the author and do not
necessarily reflect the views of the publisher, and the publisher hereby disclaims any responsibility for them.

Any people depicted in stock imagery provided by Getty Images are models,
and such images are being used for illustrative purposes only.
Certain stock imagery © Getty Images.

This book is printed on acid-free paper.

ISBN: 978-1-4969-6895-1 (sc)
ISBN: 978-1-4969-6896-8 (e)

Library of Congress Control Number: 2015902001

Print information available on the last page.

Published by AuthorHouse 10/11/2024

authorHOUSE®

THE ORANGE CHIHUAHUA

KELLY ANN GUGLIETTI

ILLUSTRATOR DWAIN ESPER

Once upon a time, near the mangroves in Mahahual, Mexico, there lived a Chihuahua named Amador. Amador was the beloved pet of Senor Pedro, a tallavera souvenir salesman. Amador and Senor Pedro did everything together. Senor Pedro took Amador to his souvenir store in town early every morning.

They would eat lunch at the docks of Puerto Costa Maya, where the cruise ships rolled in.

There, Amador would play with his friends Alita, Novia, Joles and Riz under the watchful eye of Senor Pedro.

After the store closed for the day, Senor Pedro would take Amador to the produce market on the way home.

After dinner, Senor Pedro always took off his slippers and fell asleep in his favorite stuffed chair in front of the TV. Amador curled up with his chin resting on Senor Pedro's feet, staring at Senor Pedro's slippers.

Amador, too, would fall asleep, but at the stroke of midnight,
he would jump into Senor Pedro's slippers. . . .

and as if by magic, he sprouted a black handlebar mustache, donned a garland of red chili peppers, a festive serape and sombrero and whirred through the front door out into the dark night.

"AH-AH-AHOOOOO! CHILE'S COME TO PLAY! Yip! Yip! Yeah!" Amador howled and yipped to announce his presence.

All the Chihuahuas in the town came out to party. Music, only the dogs could hear, magically appeared.

Now Chile, as Amador was known in this part of the story, was always the life of the party. He'd swoop the damsels off their feet, whether they liked it or not.

He'd dance a mean salsa.

He bellowed out with confidence when dared to do karaoke.

Large crowds relished his stories of stowing away in the purses of tourists to cruise the ports.

Many wanted to be just like Chile. How extraordinary he seemed! Soon some of Chile's admirers would try his tricks, but they did not work!

They talked to the other Chihuahuas in the neighborhood. It seemed to all that Chile was a pompous, arrogant show off. He was fascinating to listen to, but he was definitely a phony. It was agreed that Chile should be exposed for who he really was immediately.

Fortunately the next night, as Amador was resting on Senor Pedro's feet, he noticed a different pair of slippers on the floor. "Oh no!" he panicked. "What am I going to do? Senor Pedro's slippers turned me into Chile, the most popular pup in Mahahual!"

Amador jumped into Senor Pedro's new slippers to see what would happen. Nothing happened!

Amador tried to go through the front door, but bounced off it, nearly waking Senor.

Amador had to use the doggy door.

"Ah! Ah! Ahoooo! Yip! Yip! Yeah!" Amador faintly squeaked out.

"Amador?" Joles gasped in surprise. "Where is Chile?" Alita, Novia and Riz chimed in.

"Guys, there is no Chile. I made him up," confessed Amador sadly with a stammer in his voice. "It's these slippers! They don't work!" he complained. "These are Senor Pedro's NEW slippers and there is NO magic in them!" he cried.

"Amador, you silly dog! You created Chile for us?" Amador's friends laughed. "Chile was funny," Joles added. "He was weird, man!" exclaimed Riz. "Really full of himself" humphed Alita and Novia.

"Thanks for the entertainment, but we missed you," 'Joles chuckled. "We wondered why you never came to the parties. We can talk to you," expressed Riz. "We know you care about what we have to say and we care about what you have to say," sang Alita and Novia. "Man, what would YOU like to do tonight?" offered 'Joles.

"Just relax!" sighed Amador. "It's too much pressure to be like Chile all the time. I don't really get to know anyone. Let's just lie under the stars and tell cat stories. Did you hear the one about "The Green Tom?"

The moral of this story is that you will never know what is thought of you unless you are you. False images only hide your true self.

Dear Parents, Teachers and Guidance Counselors:

I hope you have enjoyed sharing this story with your child(ren) or student(s). You will find five activities on the next few pages that encourage them to think more about the story and respond to it in different ways. Feel free to pick and choose which activities you believe will fit your audience.

Catch my other books, "The Green Tom" and "The Yellow Sea Lioness." There may be more yet! Until then, best wishes for a more literate and compassionate tomorrow.

Kelly Ann Guglietti

FUN LITERACY ACTIVITY 1

What four elements made up Chile's costume?

1.

2.

3.

4.

Name four elements to a costume you can use to make yourself different.

1.

2.

3.

4.

FUN LITERACY ACTIVITY 2

Have you ever made up a story about yourself that was not true? Write about it. Tell:

How your story made you feel?
How others who heard your story felt?
If you got caught in your lie?
Were you afraid you might get caught in your lie? How did this make you feel?

Now reverse the questions:
Have you ever heard a story that you know someone made up?
How did you feel about being lied to? Did you feel like calling that person out in their lie?

Can you relax when you tell lies?

_____

_____

_____

_____

_____

_____

_____

_____

_____

_____

_____

_____

FUN LITERACY ACTIVITY 2

Have you ever made up a story about yourself that was not true? Write about it. (Continued)

_____
_____
_____
_____
_____
_____
_____
_____
_____
_____
_____
_____
_____
_____
_____
_____
_____
_____
_____

FUN LITERACY ACTIVITY 3

Amador was lucky to have his four good friends. How do you think the story would have ended if others came out to Amador's weak call for a party? Illustrate your solution and write one or two sentences describing your new ending to the story.

FUN LITERACY ACTIVITY 4

You are pretending to be someone you are not. You get caught. Draw a picture of how you feel.

FUN LITERACY ACTIVITY 5

Design a new serape and sombrero for Chile. Explain why you chose the colors you chose.

GLOSSARY

Alita – wing or guide
Amador – beloved
'Joles – short for frijoles (beans)
Novia - sweetheart
Riz - rice
Puerto - port
Senor - mister
Serape – blanket
Sombrero – Mexican hat
Tallavera – colorful glazed and decorated ceramics of Spanish or Spanish colonial origin

Printed in the United States
by Baker & Taylor Publisher Services